THE TIDY GUIDE TO PUBLISHING YOUR NOVEL

The clutter-free, 30-minute course for publishing a book the right way

RACHEL AUKES

The Tidy Guide Series by Rachel Aukes

The Tidy Guide to Writing a Novel

The Tidy Guide to Self-Editing Your Novel

The Tidy Guide to Publishing Your Novel

THE TIDY GUIDE TO PUBLISHING YOUR NOVEL

Copyright 2019 Rachel Aukes.
All rights reserved.

Reproduction in whole or part of this publication without express written consent is prohibited.

Please consider leaving a review wherever you bought the book, or telling your friends about it, to help spread the word. Thank you for supporting the author's work.

Cover Design by Evernight Designs.

Print ISBN-13: 978-1-7328449-5-7

Introduction

The landscape of the publishing world has changed. For the past century, books were printed and made available to stores as either paperbacks or hardcovers. That distribution method evolved when the e-book arrived. Stores are no longer limited by shelf space, and readers can choose from millions of books on any given day. E-books led publishers to rethink how they released books; and e-books led to the popularity of a new publishing model: self-publishing.

This Tidy Guide focuses on the two most common publishing paths: traditional publishing and self-publishing. The path you choose may be different for each novel you write. If you want to self-publish, then by all means, self-publish. Likewise, if you dream of working with a publisher, then you should follow your dream. The path is yours for the choosing.

Embrace your publishing adventure!

Choose your publishing adventure

"Publishing is a business. Writing may be art, but publishing, when all is said and done, comes down to dollars." ~ Nicholas Sparks

In today's digital age, writers have fewer barriers to publishing than ever before. Anyone with a computer and internet connection can publish a book with minimal cost.

Writers choose from two publishing paths: traditional publishing through an established publisher or self-publishing. Each path brings its own set of opportunities and challenges. You may choose a different path based on your book's subject, genre, and audience. I'm a hybrid writer, which means that I publish some of my books through publishing houses, and I publish some of my books on my own. When I write a new book, I analyze it to see if it (1) fits with a particular house, and (2) has high commercial appeal based on current or predicted trends. If it fits both criteria, I tend to use a traditional publisher. I wrote *The Deadland Saga* when the zombie trend felt saturated (and thus may have had less commercial appeal), and so I chose to self-publish; *The Colliding Worlds Trilogy* is science fiction with romantic elements, which is an evergreen niche, and I published through Simon & Schuster. I take this hybrid approach so that I can still write exactly what I want to write even if the story isn't a perfect fit for a publishing house.

Traditional publishers take a load off your shoulders

For the past century, large publishing houses come to mind when one thinks of publishing. The "Big Five" publishers are known to all readers: Penguin Random House, HarperCollins, Macmillan, Simon & Schuster, and Hachette. Dozens, if not hundreds, of imprints exist within each of these houses. An ***imprint*** is a group within the house that focuses on a specific type or genre of books, such as the Harlequin romance imprint within Harper-Collins.

The recent boom of e-books has led to a paradigm shift in publishing, wherein small, independent publishing houses have found greater opportunities for success. These houses operate much like the Big Five but produce far fewer books per year, often focusing on niche genres.

Benefits

Publishers build their reputation by producing quality books and investing in an author's career. They are selective of which stories to buy—stories not only need to be good but also a fit with the publishing house's area of focus in terms of story themes and reader demographics.

Publishers commonly pay an advance against royalties, or advance, for any story they buy, though the smallest houses—especially ones that publish only e-books and Print on Demand (POD) paperbacks—may not provide any advance. An advance is an up-front payment made to an author that is deducted from future royalties. For example, a house may offer a $5,000 advance to a writer for a book. The writer may receive $1,500 upon signing the contract, another $1,500 upon submitting the manuscript, and the final $2,000 upon publication. Once enough royalties have come in to cover the $5,000 advance, the book has "earned out" its advance, and the writer will begin to receive royalties on all future sales. Advances are largely handled in multiple payments to help the writer by providing some income up front while protecting the publisher from not having an outlay of too much cash months or years before a book is published.

Up-front income and no publishing costs are a significant benefit of working with a publisher. The publisher absorbs all publishing costs in exchange for a percentage of royalties. This model makes the publisher financially vested in the book's success.

The publisher guides the writer through the process, which can reduce the writer's stress and workload and allow the writer to remain focused on being a writer. Having a full team of professionals—editors, cover designers, and publicists—is very attractive to writers who don't want to bear the full load of publishing a book.

A benefit to working with a larger house is that you are more likely to see your book on bookstore and library shelves across the country. This visibility, coupled with visibility through the publisher's standard marketing channels, will expose your book to readers who may not see it otherwise, which in turn can open it to greater word-of-mouth promotion, reviews by major news sites, and submissions for traditional awards.

Challenges

Publishing houses ease the publishing process and bring a wealth of knowledge and experience, but that comes at a lower revenue rate for writers, which means you need to sell more copies of a traditionally published book than of a self-published book to make the same revenue. Publishers pay a **royalty**, which is a percentage of a book's net revenue, such as twenty-five percent of net revenue of each sale. Self-publishers receive the full net revenue provided by each retailer, i.e., there's no "middleman" to take a cut. However, self-publishers incur publishing costs, so the comparison of royalty rates and revenue rates is not an even comparison.

A publishing contract once meant a writer would see his or her books on bookstore shelves. In the digital age, many publishers release books as e-books and POD paperbacks, releasing fewer books widely to physical stores and libraries. A traditional publishing contract no longer guarantees you'll see your book in bookstores and libraries.

Another challenge writers face with publishers is that it can take a long time from submitting the manuscript to seeing the published book. Querying agents and editors and then publishing can each take anywhere from a few months to years. The delay in a world moving at an ever-increasing pace has led some writers to self-publish.

Self-publishing gives you complete control

Self-publishing is a business model wherein the author manages all publishing activities for their book. Writing is one job; publishing is another job. Self-publishing is an exhilarating, and sometimes exhausting, business model. If you thrive on being your own boss, then self-publishing is an option you should consider.

Benefits

Self-publishers control every aspect of the publishing process, from setting release dates to choosing book covers. Self-publishing also allows a writer to release a book that doesn't fit neatly into a particular genre or a book that a traditional publisher would have a difficult time marketing. Books published by their authors can often be released faster since the author is taking on much of the work and can engage freelance contractors who are more readily available.

Writers will see a greater percentage of revenue from books they self-publish, normally thirty to seventy percent of the retail price. The frequency of receiving revenue payments is often monthly, whereas traditional publishers may pay quarterly, semi-annually, or even annually.

And perhaps the greatest benefit of all is that when you self-publish, you retain all rights to your book. Whether those are e-book, print, audio, entertainment, or translation rights, they are available should you receive an offer from a publisher to sell at a later date.

Challenges

Self-publishing does not come without its own set of challenges, with the most notable challenge being up-front costs. Depending on your freelance team, you may have to pay for multiple editing passes, cover design, and formatting. The price ranges for every type of service vary greatly, generally based on the freelancer's level of experience and reputation. Editors often charge hundreds, sometimes over a thousand dollars, as do cover designers. Formatters typically charge fifty to two hundred dollars. If you plan to self-publish, be sure to build a budget or a plan for negotiating these services.

The time commitment involved in self-publishing is also significant. If you work a second job in addition to being a writer, you may need to spread out releases to avoid burnout. Being a publisher is a job in itself.

Because of time and cost constraints, and a lack of publishing knowledge for newer writers, a self-published title may have fewer people involved with transforming a manuscript into a book. Fewer eyes on a project potentially means more things slip through, especially during the editing phase. This is most apparent when a writer takes on nearly all tasks on his or her own. For example, if you rely only on your own skills to edit your manuscript, a plot that makes sense in your mind may not have been clearly communicated in words. Or, if you create your own cover without regard to design best practices, you may focus too much on conveying the story on the cover rather than on the right typography, colors, and standards specific to the genre in which you intend to market. If you must take on these tasks, then take extra care in ensuring you approach the tasks from the perspective of an outside professional and not of the story creator.

Since self-publishing is done by each writer, every self-published book is produced based on an individual's sense of quality. This has led to some self-published titles being released with inconsistent storylines and numerous grammatical errors and typos. These titles were especially common in the early years of Kindle, but new titles can still be found today. While fading, the perception lingers that self-published titles may be of a lower quality than traditionally published titles. This means you must ensure your book is of superior quality when it's released.

It's your name on the cover, so build a brand of excellence. With that mindset, you'll quickly build a following of passionate readers.

Assisted self-publishers manage the process for you at a cost

There are companies who will help writers publish their books for a fee. This may be a potential solution for writers who want to self-publish but don't have the time or experience to manage the publishing process. Assisted self-publishers handle the process much like a traditional publisher would with one significant difference: for publishing houses, the *reader* is the customer; for assisted self-publishers, the *writer* is the customer. This means that assisted self-publishers have no vested interest in the success of your book—they only care about the production of your book.

Be *very* careful in working with an assisted self-publisher. Some are considered vanity publishers, which are predatory assisted self-publishers. Vanity publishers not only charge writers for their services but also claim rights to the books. If you work with an assisted self-publisher, make sure:

- You keep *all* rights to your work, without exception. Assisted self-publishers produce books, distribute them across retailers, and manage revenue payments. They should not require you to sign away any rights to your story.
- You receive all net book revenue. If you pay up front, an assisted self-publisher should not take a percent of your book's revenue as well *unless* you are paying them a commission to manage payments and tax forms for you.
- The production agreement includes a termination clause. Any assisted self-publisher should agree to terminate the agreement and unpublish your books if you provide a written notice. If you do not see a termination clause, don't walk, run away from that publisher.
- You keep all book files, including cover and

interior formats, if you end the agreement. You paid for your book's production—you own these files.

A reputable assisted self-publisher will produce a professional-quality book with you at a fair price. They live by their reputation and by repeat customers. Vanity publishers try to make as much money off a writer during the first book since most writers would never want to use their services again. Do your research. If prices for their service seems high, or if they constantly try to up-sell additional services to you, they are likely a vanity publisher. Organizations such as the Alliance of Independent Authors (ALLi) lists recommended assisted self-publishers. And websites such as Writer Beware and Absolute Write Water Cooler provide opinions on publishers and known predatory publishers.

Other paths may lead to publishing

If you do not wish to take either the traditional publishing or self-publishing route, there are other paths that may lead to revenue and even your book on retailer sites. The online posting of stories, often in serialized format, remains ever popular. Wattpad, Radish, and personal blogs are common places for posting stories in an online format. Radish allows paid content so writers can make money from their stories, and Wattpad's breakout hits have led to publishing and movie deals.

Patreon is another popular site for selling online content wherein a writer's patrons pay a monthly fee for exclusive content. Some writers have used Patreon to build an audience and a publishing budget.

You have responsibilities regardless of the path you choose

Regardless of the publishing path you choose, a solid story wrapped in a polished manuscript is crucial to a good published book. In manufacturing, they call this the "garbage in, garbage out" rule. If your story was hastily typed without regard to the fundamentals of plot, characterization, world-building, and structure, then no matter how much you spend and how much work you put into the publishing process, your book will never be as good as it could've been.

Don't choose self-publishing because one hundred publishers rejected your story. Rejections may mean a story is not a good fit for a house, but they may also mean there's a serious flaw in the story. Self-publishing should be a primary plan, not a backup plan. Choose self-publishing because you believe it's the right publishing path for your story, whether that's because you want revenue, exposure, or experience.

Regardless of how you publish, book promotion falls squarely on your shoulders. While traditional publishing houses will help with some marketing, don't expect a nationwide book tour unless your publisher thinks your book will be a #1 *New York Times* best seller. Learning how to actively market your books will help you throughout your career.

All publishing, regardless of the path you choose, involves work and commitment from marketing to meeting deadlines. When you approach publishing as an engaged professional, you're sure to succeed.

Your intellectual rights are yours to keep or sell

You created your story. You own all rights to that story unless you sign those rights to someone else in a contract. Every book has several types of rights you can sell. These include publishing rights for print, e-book, and audio; entertainment rights for media, film, games, and more; and territory rights for countries and languages.

No one can publish or make money off your work without your permission. Guard your rights, as they can be highly valuable. Never sign away rights for free, and never sign away rights without a reversion clause.

The traditional publishing path

When you publish through a traditional publisher, you have the benefit of seasoned professionals guiding and helping you through the process. You are an integral part of the process, and the more engaged you are, the better chance your book has for success.

The difference between literary agents and acquisitions editors

Many writers who traditionally publish have agents represent their stories to editors. A ***literary agent*** is an industry professional who represents a writer and their stories to publishers, film studios, and other venues who produce entertainment based on stories. An agent receives a percentage (generally fifteen percent in the United States) of the writer's profits received from publishers. An agent *never* charges a writer to represent them. Many large publishers won't accept submissions directly from writers, so a writer needs an agent to submit on their behalf.

Some publishers, especially small or new houses, don't

require writers to be agented. These publishers allow writers to submit directly to their acquisitions editors. An ***acquisitions editor*** is an editor whose job is to buy, or acquire, rights to literary works for their publisher.

Acquiring a literary agent

If you do not have an agent and wish to have one represent you, these are the standard steps:

1. Select agent(s) to query. Learn about agents by talking with other writers or researching online.
2. Submit a query, per the guidelines listed on the agent's website. A ***query*** is a brief letter that describes your story. Many queries also include a ***synopsis***, which is a narrative outline of your story.
3. If the agent is interested in learning more, they will contact you to request additional material. Often, the agent may request a ***partial***, which is the first few pages or chapters of your story, or a ***full***, which is the complete manuscript.
4. If the agent wishes to represent you, they will make you an ***offer of representation***, which covers how they will represent and support you and for what percentage fee.

You may bypass the second step if you meet an agent online or at a conference and they ask you to send your story to them.

Once you have an agent, they will represent you and your story to publishers and work on your behalf to ensure you get the best deal possible. Selling your work to a publisher is very similar to acquiring an editor.

Submit to publishers that are a fit for your story

If you have an agent, they will talk with you about which publishers they'd like to submit your story to. If you are querying publishers' acquisitions editors directly, you may need to do a little research. Look at books in the same genre as your story and see who published them. Many genres have their own professional writer organizations, such as Romance Writers of America (RWA), Horror Writers Association (HWA), and Science Fiction and Fantasy Writers of America (SFWA). Writer organizations often maintain lists of recommended publishers. Once you make a list of publishers which you'd like to query, review their submission guidelines.

Some publishers do not allow simultaneous submissions, which means you should not submit to anyone else during the time they are reviewing your submission. Prioritize your publishers and be patient after you submit your query.

Your query submission to publishers is often the same format agents request: a brief letter with story description, a synopsis, and/or a partial or full manuscript.

Editors may ask for partial, full, or revise-and-resubmit manuscripts

Just like querying agents, acquisitions editors may reach out to you for additional information before either rejecting the story or offering you a contract for rights to that story. Editors will request a partial or full manuscript if they didn't request it as part of the submission process. They may also request a ***revise-and-resubmit***, which occurs when they like the story, but there's something significant to the story that doesn't work. This could be a lack of characterization, plot holes, or something else. When this happens, the editor will point out what didn't work for them. It's your choice then to make changes and resubmit the manuscript. Fulfilling a revise-and-resubmit request does not guarantee a contract; it only guarantees the editor will take a second look at your story.

The magical moment when you're offered a contract

You'll always remember the exciting moment when you receive "the call" from your agent or the acquisitions editor. They want your story! But don't sign the contract right away (even though you want to). If you have an agent, their area of expertise is negotiating the contract to be as beneficial to you as possible. After all, their pay is dependent on your success. If you don't have an agent and desperately want one, you can email an agent with your contract offer in hand to see if they'll represent you, at least for that story. Without an agent, you're on your own for negotiating the contract, but you don't have to be. You can have an attorney—one who specializes in literary, entertainment, or intellectual property—review the contract for you.

The contract will detail which right(s) the publisher wishes to buy, such as e-book, print, or audio rights; media rights; game rights; language rights; world rights; and other rights. What you get paid depends on which rights you're selling, your level of fame, and your book's forecasted success.

One tip in negotiating your contract: ensure the contract includes a ***reversion clause***. This clause details how you can get your rights back under certain criteria, usually after a certain length of time. Without a reversion clause, the publisher owns forever the rights you've sold to your story.

What happens after you sign the contract

After you sign the contract, your agent and the publisher's acquisitions editor will walk you through their publishing process and timeline for your book. You'll likely be assigned an editor who will be your point person throughout the entire editing process, which may include rounds of developmental (or content) edits, line edits, copy edits, and proofreading.

Your editor will be your main contact at the publisher, but they will not be the only person you'll work with within the house. You'll have an entire team focused on preparing your book for publication, including multiple editors, a cover designer, a publicist, and possibly more. Smaller houses may have team members perform multiple roles.

The publishing process may feel lengthy, but many activities are taking place. The first set of activities are focused on editing the manuscript, which can take multiple rounds and months of going back and forth with editors.

During the editing process, other activities kick off. A cover designer will create the book cover based on input from the editor and writer. Note that the writer rarely has final approval of the cover—the publisher does because they want the cover to mesh into their overall catalog and demographic.

The book's publicist develops a publicity plan for the book release. The amount of marketing and promotion provided by a publisher varies by the book and writer. An author with a history of bestsellers will receive a far greater promotional budget than a debut author. All writers are expected to promote their own book besides the support a publisher provides, so the next 30-minute course, *The Tidy Guide to Marketing Your Novel*, will cover ideas for you on review copies, ads, newsletters, social media, and more.

One promotional item created for most books is the **Advance Reader Copy (ARC)**, which is an early copy (sometimes not yet proofed) that the writer and publisher can provide to reviewers and other sources for early word-of-mouth promotion.

As the release date approaches, the book files will be formatted, the book description will be finalized, and your author biography will be needed. All the hard work culminates in a professionally released book that makes you (hopefully) proud.

The self-publishing path

When you self-publish, you must change your perspective from writer to publisher. You must remove yourself from the story and instead focus on creating a product that is both attractive and easily accessible to readers. When you are a self-publisher, you are competing with all other publishers for readers' attention. That means that the quality of your product must meet or exceed what is produced by traditional publishing houses to stand out.

What self-publishing is and is not

Self-publishing is a valid form of publishing. It is not a substandard form of publishing—a self-published book can be as good of quality as a traditionally published book. However, self-publishing *can* be a substandard form of publishing if you don't put forth the same effort and attention that publishing houses display. We've all seen "those" books: the ones riddled with errors or wrapped in "homemade" covers. I'm not saying you can't design your own cover, but if you design your own book cover, make sure you follow best practices in cover design for your genre.

Uploading a book to an aggregator or to a retailer, such as Amazon, has been easy in recent years. Just because hitting the "Publish" button is easy doesn't mean you should skimp on any steps. Doing so will bring you many heartaches and fewer sales on both the current and future books.

Your success as a self-publisher falls on your shoulders, but you're not in it alone: you'll have a support team of editors, cover designers, beta readers, and so on. But no one on your support team has the level of ownership you have in being a successful self-publisher.

Set a release schedule that won't run you ragged

The first publishing decision I make for a novel is to set a release date. This is as simple as writing a date on a sticky note and placing it on my computer. The reason I set my release date before I start all my other publishing activities is because the date gives me something to work backward from. I've self-published over a dozen novels and have found a release schedule of minimum dates required for each release activity. That means, when I hire someone—an editor, for example—I expect them to need at least a two-week turnaround time.

The timeline displayed below is the generic release schedule of *minimum* turnaround times I work from in planning each book's release. I've listed all the major activities in publishing a book along with the minimum time required for each activity. Note that this timeline does not include marketing activities, which is an entire process on its own and will be covered in *The Tidy Guide to Marketing Your Novel* (coming late 2019).

This is an aggressive timeline for the first-time self-publisher, and you'd likely want to *at least* double all the minimum timing estimates. After you have a couple books published and have an established team, you'll find your own rhythm and what works better for you and your team.

An example self-publishing timeline					
Plan	Create Cover		Send ARCs	Format files	Publish book
	Edit	Proofread			
1 day	2 weeks	1 week	2 weeks	1 day	1 day — Release Day

Every writer will develop a slightly different release schedule in terms of activities and/or timing. For example, I format my own book files. If I hired that activity out, then I would need to allot a week or longer for that activity. Or, some writers include content edits before copy edits for an additional, third round of edits. Or, some writers want the audiobook released at the same time as the e-book and paperback. If this is the case, you must add on at least another month for audiobook creation.

Which activities you do yourself and which activities you hire out depends on your skills, time availability, and budget. Since I have worked around technology much of my career, I find formatting book files a breeze. But when I designed three of my book covers for *The Deadland Saga*, I found I'd burned hours upon hours in getting the covers to where I was satisfied. I've hired out covers ever since, because time is often my biggest constraint on a book launch. I also hire an editor and a proofreader to ensure my manuscript is as ready as it can be for publication.

Note that every contractor you hire is working on other books, so the earlier you can get on their calendar, the better chance you have at not having to push back your release date. It is not uncommon for editors and cover designers to be booked at least six months in advance.

Also keep in mind that many activities are dependent on the activity before it being completed. You can't proofread your manuscript without it first being edited, you can't upload your book files until they are formatted, and so on.

By setting the release date first, I've sometimes had to go back to change it. Usually, this was because the date did not work with a freelancer's schedule. This is why I never create a book for pre-order on Amazon without first having my team assembled and all working from the same release date.

Let's look at the generic release schedule using dates. For example, if I set a release date of July 1, I need the minimum time listed for each activity, I would need to begin my publishing activities by or before May 24. This example assumes a perfect-case scenario, where each activity takes exactly the amount of days and weeks I estimated in my generic timeline above and all contractors could fit my schedule. It also doesn't take into account any holidays, such as the U. S. Memorial Day, or other time off you need as a human.

Starting with July 1 and working backward, I now have "start by" dates for each activity. If I'm working with a contractor, my "start by" date is the date they tell me they need it to be.

An example self-publishing calendar

25	26	27	28	29	30	31
			Create cover			
			Edit			
01	02	03	04	05	06	07
			Create cover			
			Edit			
08	09	10	11	12	13	14
			Create cover			
			Proofread			
15	16	17	18	19	20	21
			Send out ARCs			
22	23	24	25	26	27	28
			Send out ARCs			
29	30	01	02	03	04	
Format files	Publish book					

(Plan: 24)

Once every contractor is confirmed, it's time to make the release date official. Add it to your calendar. Use a countdown timer to build excitement. Tell your family and friends, because a book launch is always cause for celebration.

Now, let's dig into each of these major self-publishing activities…

You have a wealth of distribution options

Book formats

When you publish, you choose from a variety of formats, with e-book, print, and audiobook being the three most common formats. E-book is the simplest of the formats. Many distributors can accept and convert a clean Microsoft Word file, so you don't even need to create the .EPUB or similar format yourself. But having a clean file is key. This means you need to use "styles" so that a chapter title is the "Heading 1" style and the content is the "Normal" style. Without styles, the conversion software won't know the difference between chapter headings and the body of the chapter. If you're not comfortable with Word styles, you may want to consider hiring a formatter.

Print is slightly more complicated in that distributors require a PDF format that displays the novel exactly how it should look in print. Many distributors offer free Word templates to help make formatting easier. As with e-books, hire a formatter if you're not comfortable with styles, margins, and page sizes.

Producing an audiobook is the most challenging of the formats, as you either need to work with an audiobook performer to narrate your book, or you need a sound booth to produce a professional-sounding product. There are fewer retailers for audiobooks, but the number is growing every year.

Book retailers and aggregators

Once you choose the format(s), you then choose how best to distribute the novel. There are three types of vendors who distribute your book. **Retailers** are stores that sell books, such as Amazon or Barnes & Noble. ***Aggregators*** distribute your book—whether that's e-book, print, or audiobook—to a range of retailers. **Distributors** are a subset of aggregators that, for a small percentage fee, focus on distributing print books to retailers and libraries; though "distributor" is also used as a generic term to refer to all retailers and aggregators. Many aggregators fulfill the role of distributor as well, so it can be confusing. For simplicity's sake, we'll focus on retailers and aggregators as book distributors as a whole.

For e-books, the biggest decision is whether you want to have your book available only through a single retailer—i.e. Amazon via its Kindle Direct Publishing (KDP) "Select"—or have your book available through multiple retailers, i.e. "wide." ***Going wide*** means your book could be available via Kobo, Google Play, Barnes & Noble, Apple Books, and more. These retailers have self-publishing portals to make it easy for you to publish your book to their store.

Amazon KDP Select includes access to the popular Kindle Unlimited (KU) subscription library, which *can* be a significant portion of e-book revenue. However, KDP Select requires exclusivity for ninety days. First-time publishers often first release their e-book to Amazon only via KDP Select for simplicity, but the Amazon vs. wide decision is a personal decision.

If you choose to go wide, you may consider an aggregator to simplify the publishing process. These online self-publishing sites help you build your e-book, and they then make it available to many retailers, libraries, and subscription services for a small percentage fee. Using an aggregator, you only have to upload your book once rather than uploading it to every separate retailer. Smashwords and Draft2Digital are the two largest aggregators, with IngramSpark, BookBaby, and others filling in a significant portion of the remaining market.

Many retailers and aggregators offer the ability to sell both e-book and print, making it easier for the writer to publish multiple formats. Several offer audiobook services, such as Draft2Digital's interface with Findaway Voices.

Metadata

Understanding your book's **metadata** will help you pull together all the information retailers and aggregators ask for. Metadata refers to any details that help identify your book in the ocean of books. Think of metadata as terms a customer may search for in looking for a book to buy. The most common metadata include your book's title, subtitle, ISBN, description, genre/categories, keywords, age/grade demographic, format, release date, and retail price.

You'll need much of this information if you hire a cover designer. For example, the book description will be listed on the back of the print cover. Other metadata, such as the genre and reader demographic, can assist the cover designer in ensuring your book's cover conveys the right message to your target audience.

Note that ISBNs (International Standard Book Numbers) are used on print books in the United States. You do not need an ISBN for either e-books or audiobooks. Many retailers and aggregators offer a free ISBN, but if you use their ISBN, they will be listed as the publisher on record. This means that if you set up your print book on Amazon KDP and use their provided ISBN, Amazon will be listed as the publisher even when the book is sold to bookstores or libraries. If you do not want this, you must buy your ISBNs through Bowker, which is the only provider of ISBNs in the United States. I buy my own ISBNs so that my personal imprint (Waypoint Books) is listed as the publisher and to ensure I own all aspects of that book. Publishing is a business, and I believe that the more pieces of the business I control the better.

A perk of self-publishing is that you can change the retail price of your book any time. Some writers will launch their book at a temporarily reduced price; other writers launch at full price. Your launch pricing depends on your launch marketing strategy, which I'll cover in *The Tidy Guide to Marketing Your Novel*.

Readers do judge a book by its cover

A book cover piques a reader's interest in learning more about a book. Having a professional-grade cover that represents both the genre and your story is crucial to sales.

If you have experience in graphic design and have the right software, then you may consider doing your own cover. Otherwise, I highly recommend you hire a cover designer.

A ***cover designer*** uses a variety of stock digital images and photographs and typography to create a cover that helps your novel stand out in its genre.

Most covers are created using stock images, as there are so many available at reasonable prices. When stock images are used on your cover, you have purchased rights to using that image; you have not purchased that image. That means you may see the same image used on other covers.

Some writers hire a ***cover artist*** to draw their cover from scratch. Having a unique cover means you'll never see the same image on another cover, but it will also cost more.

There are many high-quality cover designers available. One way to find a cover designer is to look at the copyright page of a book with a cover you like. Cover designers are often listed, especially on self-published books. Or, you can reach out to a writer to ask them who did their cover. Note that writers published through a large house may not know who their designer is, as they are more removed from the process.

To save costs, some cover designers offer premade covers for writers to buy. When a writer selects one of these covers, the designer will add the title, your author name, and other text details to personalize the cover. If you buy a premade cover, be sure that it fits the story. For example, if your heroine is blonde on the cover but brunette in the story, readers will notice.

If your publishing budget is tight, I recommend

splurging on the cover. There are other ways to save money on the remaining publishing activities, but your book cover is often a potential reader's first impression of your story.

Engage an editor to make your story shine

Few writers can objectively edit their story. They are too close to the words. A fresh pair of eyes can make the difference between a story riddled with errors and a story that holds on to readers and never lets them go.

Depending on your needs, you may want to engage a developmental editor (also known as a content editor), a copyeditor, a proofreader, or any combination of the three main types. Costs increase the deeper the edits. A proofreading, which is scanning a work for typographical errors, is cheaper than copyediting, which is reviewing each sentence. Content edits deep dive into plot and characterization and run the most expensive.

Critique partners, who are often fellow writers, can also help point out flaws in a story, potentially cutting editing expenses. To further reduce your editing costs, self-edit your work as much as possible. Read to *The Tidy Guide to Self-Editing Your Novel* for details on the self-editing process and tips for working with an editor.

Build an army of beta readers

Just as some customers enjoy trying out beta apps to get an insider view, beta readers are voracious readers who enjoy reading pre-release copies of books. These copies, also called Advance Reader Copies, or ARCs, have been edited but may not be fully proofed or formatted yet. ARCs are often sent as PDFs, though many writers also make them available in Kindle and .EPUB formats.

Beta readers often receive free early copies in exchange for reviews and word-of-mouth promotion when the book is published. Some beta readers even provide feedback and point out typos and other errors or inconsistencies they've found.

Beta readers are hard to find for new writers. As you publish more books, you'll build an army of beta readers who love reading your stories. If you have an email newsletter or social media presence, reach out to your followers and ask for beta readers. Even if you have only one or two beta readers for your first book's release, that could mean one or two reviews on release day, which could give your book a jump start ahead of other books with no reviews.

Book formats need to be easy on the eyes

Formatting e-books and print books can be easy. As I mentioned earlier, if you have a clean document, you can upload it directly to retailers and aggregators, who then build the e-book for you. Draft2Digital is known for their free, easy, and customizable e-book setup which produces e-book formats you can download and use for any retailers and for personal use, such as review copies.

There are also software tools available for formatting e-books and print books. I use Vellum, but it requires a Mac operating system. If you choose not to format your own book, formatters are the least expensive of all publishing contractors and can often provide book files within days.

Audiobooks are a different thing since the book is produced as an audio file rather than as a text file. If you hire someone to produce your audiobook, you'll be asked to provide audio notes that include details on major characters and pronunciation of unique words. For example, on every set of audiobook notes, I mention how to pronounce my last name, which is pronounced differently than most assume (it's pronounced *Ah-kess*). If you produce your own audiobook, you'll need audio software to create the audio files that split chapters into separate files.

Clicking the "publish" button is an exhilarating activity

When you have your final book files, you've reached the most exciting part of the self-publishing process, and that's uploading your files and clicking "Publish."

Be sure to finish setting up your book and submit your book files at least one day before your planned release date. This is because many retailers take twelve to twenty-four hours to list your book in their store. Aggregators often take longer because they need to send your book to the various retailers who then upload to their stores.

If you set your book up for pre-order, note that Amazon requires the final book files to be submitted *at least* three days before release date. I recommend you build in a buffer and upload files well before the deadline, or you could risk seeing a draft book file available for sale.

Many retailers allow you to save a draft of your book, so you can set it up as soon as you have your metadata. I take this approach with all my books so I have less to worry about right before the release date when marketing activities can be chaotic.

Even if you choose to distribute your book via an aggregator, such as Smashwords or Draft2Digital, you may still want to distribute your book directly via Amazon KDP. Amazon is the largest source of e-book revenue for many writers, so most choose to distribute directly to Amazon via KDP rather than through an aggregator to keep the highest percentage of revenue.

A published book changes your life

"Once you publish a book, it is out of your control. You cannot dictate how people read it." ~ Margaret Atwood

Having a book published is one of the greatest joys a writer can experience. Making money from my art is great, but sharing my stories with the world brings a surreal sense of pride that never fades. Knowing that my stories bring joy to readers in countries I've never visited inspires me to improve my craft and publishing practices.

Seeing your book on sale at your favorite retailer is a culmination of months, if not years, of hard work. I encourage you to take the story you've written into the publishing process. Publishing, just like writing, takes time and energy, but I promise you that the effort and frustration will all be worth it on release day.

Tamp down any fears or insecurities you have about the publishing process and jump in. You won't regret it.

See your story published.

Then on to the next book!

Message from the author:

This is the third Tidy Guide in a series of 30-minute reads that cover writing, editing, publishing, and marketing books as well as managing your authorial career.

If you would take two minutes to post a review, I would be very grateful. If you write a review, email me at Rachel@RachelAukes.com and I will add you to a list of advance readers for the next book in the series. You will receive a free early e-copy in return for a review.

Thank you,
~ Rachel

Appendix A. The Publishing Lifecycle

1. Query agents* and/or editors
2. Submit partial or full manuscript, as requested
3. Receive offer of representation* or contract
4. Review, negotiate, and sign contract
5. Make developmental edits to manuscript
6. Make line edits to manuscript
7. Make copy edits to manuscript
8. Proofread manuscript
9. Plan publicity for book release
10. Create cover(s) for e-book and print
11. Create Advance Reader Copy (ARC) for reviewers
12. Format book files (e-book, print)
13. Celebrate release day

Note: Steps 9–11 likely take place in parallel to editing steps 5–8.

*Agents aren't required for all publishing houses. Some

publishers allow writers to query editors directly. If you do not have an agent and wish to acquire one, you'll follow the first three steps. Then, once you sign an offer of representation with an agent, the agent will represent you and guide you through the full publishing life cycle.

Appendix B. Book Launch Checklist for Self-Publishers

1. Determine book distribution options (Amazon vs. wide; e-book, print, audio) and draft metadata
2. Set tentative release date
3. Engage cover designer to create book cover
4. Engage editor(s) to edit and proofread manuscript
5. Set firm release date
6. Plan marketing activities for launch
7. Send Advance Reader Copies (ARCs) to beta readers
8. Format book files (e-book, paperback)
9. Publish book to retailers and/or aggregators
10. Celebrate release day

Also by Rachel Aukes

Fringe Series

Fringe Runner

Fringe Station

Fringe Campaign

Fringe War

Fringe Legacy

Colliding Worlds Trilogy

Collision

Implosion

Explosion

The Deadland Saga

100 Days in Deadland

Deadland's Harvest

Deadland Rising

Guardians of the Seven Seals

Knightfall

Hellbound

Standalone Fiction

Stealing Fate

About the Author

Rachel Aukes is the award-winning author of *100 Days in Deadland*, which made Suspense Magazine's Best of the Year list. She is also a Wattpad Star, her stories having over six million reads. When not writing, she can be found flying old airplanes across the Midwest countryside and catering to an exceptionally spoiled fifty-pound lapdog.

Join Rachel's readers club to get early access to new releases, sign up for contests, and receive free stuff: www.rachelaukes.com/newsletter

www.ingramcontent.com/pod-product-compliance
Lightning Source LLC
Chambersburg PA
CBHW052038070526
44584CB00020B/3147